Write Until You Feel Better

Journal Prompts for Writing through Grief and Depression

Garrett Drew Ellis

Garrett Drew Ellis
Millersville, PA 17551
www.garrettdrewellis.com

Book Layout © 2019 BookDesignTemplates.com

Write Until You Feel Better/ Garrett Drew Ellis. -- 1st ed.
ISBN 9781697441277

To each and every person alive who has ever found themselves lost in the deep.

Grief is the place where love lost its object of affection.
Depression is mist on a mirror. Clouded vision.
When love has no place to go and the world around us cannot be clearly
seen, our voice reminds us that there is still a light inside.

Garrett Drew Ellis

Contents

Introduction

"I can shake off everything as I write; my sorrows disappear, my courage is reborn."
Anne Frank

Often, I find myself bound to my bed with no desire to get out of it. Sweaty, wide awake and generally sad, I've cultivated a habit of keeping the covers tucked underneath my chin with my face turned towards the blank wall.

If I am not in bed, I am in the bathroom. I sit on the toilet with the lid down, children pawing at the door to get in. If not the bathroom, the car is the next viable option. I park it in the garage and either sit in silence or put on something sad and melodramatic. Adele's second album, Sarah McLachlan's Mirror Ball, etc. I isolate, trying to find a place where I can be alone and where noise and people and responsibility can't expose to the world how bad my situation really is.

On the worst days, none of these escapes are available. These are the days when my biochemicals are wildly out of balance. When tears fall for no reason at all and I am easily, easily frustrated.

"Drew, what's wrong? Talk to me! Please, tell me how I can help you!"

I overwhelm my wife. my family calls and I don't answer. I have even had a friend enter my darkened home unannounced, walk into my bedroom and try to pull me out of the bed. I ignored him in silence.

Years ago, I watched my mother die violently at my feet when I was 7 years old. At age 20, I watched my grandmother succumb to Parkinson's Disease. I saw my closest cousin, who was more like a sister, die in her early 30's from health issues she carried almost all of her life and watched my grandfather die from cancer. I buried and eulogized my dear, single father and began a career as an end of life doula, a career that carries the suffering and loss of others, when I was 37 years old.

I know the depths of what it means to lose people you love. In addition to a mental health diagnosis and condition that causes me to feel inherently, I also know visceral loss. To feel as if someone has taken a blunt steak knife and cut a hole into your chest. When my mother died, my grief consumed me in such an astounding and overwhelming way that I did not speak for many months and attempted suicide many times.

The long and lonely days of depression and grief are the days when nothing consoles and nothing helps. The world is grey and foggy, and I feel lost in it. I feel abandoned.

My therapist says that it is those days that I must rely on something outside of myself, something larger: God, friends or something else. Underneath his clinical vocabulary, I am convinced that he means that I should rely on medications (something I am not opposed to and that I do believe in). But I also know that on or off medication, my body usually needs something more. I pray and I lean on my faith and that too is a deep consolation. But again, the body often wants something it can touch.

So, I write. I curse and cry and bemoan my fate on paper. I imagine better days where the world my heart desires to live in is a reality. I get out a notebook or a journaling app or my laptop and allow whatever I need to say to come out.

I write poetry.

I write prayers and laments and long existential monologues between the person I am and the person I wish I was.

I scribble down musings about the end and memories about the past.

I record daydreams.
I transcribe secrets.

On those bad days when nothing else seems available, I have learned that I can entrust my heart to a crisp, blank, white page of paper. The constant flow of my fingers across the keys of my computer helps me to drop into a contemplative state, one where my thoughts are clearer and where I can hear how selfish and stupid my pity party may really be. The page doesn't speak back in the way of sharing advice. If anything, it places my words onto the surface of a mirror and shows me my face and where I am.

Now, my life as a scribe does not always make the dark days go away. In fact, it never does. What it does is give enough clarity to believe that although tears fall by the bucketful all night long, joy really is coming when the sun rises. And if not the next sun, then maybe the one after that. Maybe even at the final one.

Writing can calm the nerves enough to promote rational thinking; it comforts a soul in deep grief. I have come to appreciate my writing practice so much because it is not a solution for my depression but more of a coping mechanism. In the world of helps, there are many therapeutic techniques that can be used to ease discomfort and pain and I encourage the use of any that do so. For me, writing is one that gives color and life when I feel I have neither.

Write Until You Feel Better: *Journal Prompts for Writing Through Grief and Depression* is my first attempt to share a practice that is deeply sacred to me. I have met God during times of putting pen to paper and they have been a trusted friend when I find myself in the deep hold of depression, grief, anxiety and loneliness. I was clinically diagnosed with major depression at a very young age but did nothing to address it in its entirety until I was 30 years old. This ran in tandem with deep experiences with grief. Having ignored both for so long, I was lucky that I learned the art of journaling as a source of healing when I was young as well (more on that later). If I had not done so, I truly believe that I would have fallen victim to the permanent effects that unaddressed mental health diagnoses can bring. In other words, it saved my life.

Instead of something that is long winded and full of impracticalities, I offer this collection of prompts and musings as a jumpstart to a practice in therapeutic. Meant to inspire the pen in moments of deep darkness and sadness, I want this simple, straightforward book to be something useful. A refuge of sorts.

For this reason, I do not offer tips on writing technique. Whether you use a laptop or a journal, correct grammar or imaginative and nonsensical language, the choice is up to you. (Honestly, I suggest that you ignore technique altogether. This practice isn't meant to be an avenue toward publication. It is meant to heal.)

Personally, I use both a paper and electronic journal and if I am writing solely for my own eyes, ignore all rules of grammar. But whatever is easiest and most importantly, accessible, is the best route for you to follow.

I do want to make a few suggestions on how to use this book.

When you choose a prompt, stick with it for a predetermined amount of time. The nature of depression lends itself to feelings and words that are sometimes superficial. Additionally, grief can force you to see only what is most immediate. Dedicate yourself to a prompt for at least 15-20 min and you will find that things that you might not have been thinking about or feeling may come to the surface.

Do not let your hand stop moving. Don't give into the idea that your initial reaction to a prompt is all that you have to say about it. Studies on freewriting and stream-of-consciousness show that deep levels of change happen when we allow our writing to be continuous and without restraint.

Know that these prompts are just suggestions. Although one of these may jumpstart your writing session, your heart may go in a totally different direction. Let it be. Be open to organic freedom because it is more important that you release the built-up emotional tension rather than produce a beautifully crafted piece of writing. You are your primary audience. Write as you will.

At the same time, consistency is key. In my experience, having a regular time of writing helps to keep the unwanted emotion from overflowing. For you, that might mean writing daily or it may mean writing weekly.

Because grief and depression are close cousins and at times, may look very similar, the prompts shared here are not labeled as addressing each individually. You will not find a section on "grief" and a section on "depression". I think these prompts will serve you well because they are lumped together and address each need concurrently.

Each section however is loosely gathered into categories labeled "Quotes", "Lists", etc. Each begins with an essay about my personal experience with grief, depression, writing from quotes, etc. While my hope is that these would be helpful and edifying for you, I desire that you would engage with them as you will. Feel free to ignore, embrace, critique or find encouragement in them.

As you engage with each prompt, some of them will be singular words and others will be quotes or longer sayings. Some may have suggestions as to how to engage and still others will ask you a very short, simple question or invite you to make a list. This variety is available to you so that you may explore all that is within. And maybe, just maybe, it will inspire you to address needs that you did not know you had.

So, grab something to write on and hop in. Use a prompt a day if you are experiencing a particularly heavy season or skim through and fall upon something that speaks to you in the moment. Use this as you will, knowing that it is always readily available. Write until you feel better.

Quotes: *Writing for Clear Thinking*

> *I understood myself only after I destroyed myself. And only in the process of fixing myself did I know who I really was.*

Sade Andria Zabala

If I had a nickel for every program, coping mechanism or tool I have used to address my depression, I would have a lot of nickels. In high school, I chased busyness and false popularity. In college, it was drinking and Zen meditation and psychic readings. Right after that, I became zealously and fundamentally religious. While my faith is still even now the foremost motivating factor in my life, I recognize that at one time, I used it falsely, covering up my pain with spiritual jargon, activity and rhetoric.

In my late 20's and early 30's, I chose isolation, even amidst maintaining a family. I am 37 right now and while writing has always been a practice that kept me sane and "centered", even in the throes of my depression and damaging coping mechanisms, in the past I never depended on it the way that I currently do. I chose other things. I knew that writing was my "thing" but didn't really know. Now, it is not simply a way of prayer for me. It is THE way to pray.

For most of my life, depression has clouded my vision. Muddled my thinking. It has caused me to not see things, especially good things, for what they were or are. My mind has always been either too full of whacked-out chemical imbalances or packed with a million different thoughts. None of these had any order to them or could be understood.

Depression does that to a person. A combination of the chemical imbalances as well as the environmental/situational/relational conflicts we experience makes our depressive times feel like the thickest of fog. For me, my brain literally hurts. Migraines rack my body with pain and I physically cannot focus or think. Even when people or situations present themselves with logical outcomes and arguments, the heaviness of depression can cause us not to understand or see.

I don't know if it is the stubbornness or the "settling" that comes with approaching midlife but in the past year or so, I have seen the value in clear, functional thinking. I have learned to comprehend the chapter of a book or read a quote on social media through the lens of commitment to mental health and clarity; to slow down for a second and really consider what I just read, hopefully without the clouds that come with turbulent emotions. I have realized and learned, deeply and with much commitment, that writing is the coping mechanism for which I was built.

When we think and talk about using therapeutic writing as a means of engaging the emotions and experiences, albeit grief, depression or something else, I believe that what we are really searching for is light. Clarity. We are looking for something that will dispel shadows and bring what we are feeling (and maybe, our next steps, into view).

I once read somewhere that one of the purposes of quoting something/someone or of reading a quote is as a means of insight and to invoke philosophical opinions or opinions. It is also, and I think more importantly, to "illuminate meaning".

So, I often stop and rewrite a quote or journal my thoughts about it, before acting or deciding on a course of action. Before actively engaging my depression, I had an intellectual knowledge that a writing practice was available to me. Now, I realize that if I really want to see myself clearly, to see the world clearly and not solely through depressed eyes, I must know no other way to live.

Take these quotes as an offering. They, or some other healing modality, may be the practice for which you were born to live as well. I offer these quotes as opportunities where you may be able to see, think and write, clearly. My hope is that as you begin to cultivate a practice of clear thinking, some of the fog may lift and you may write towards that which would alleviate some of your pain.

"Every man has his secret sorrows which the world knows not; and often times we call a man cold when he is only sad."
Henry Wadsworth Longfellow

What are your secret sorrows?

"In addition to my other numerous acquaintances, I have one more intimate confidant... My depression is the most faithful mistress I have known — no wonder, then, that I return the love."
Søren_Kierkegaard

Why?

"Man is fond of counting his troubles, but he does not count his joys. If he counted them up as he ought to, he would see that every lot has enough happiness provided for it."
Fyodor Dostoevsky

Count your Joys.

"The greatest degree of inner tranquility comes from the development of love and compassion. The more we care for the happiness of others, the greater is our own sense of well-being."
Tenzin Gyatso

How can you develop your compassion?

"Start by doing what's necessary; then do what's possible; and suddenly you are doing the impossible."
St. Francis of Assisi

What is necessary?

"Depression is a prison where you are both the suffering prisoner and the cruel jailer."

Dorothy Rowe

How are you both at the same time?

"Have patience with all things, but chiefly have patience with yourself. Do not lose courage in considering your own imperfections but instantly set about remedying them — every day begin the task anew."

Saint Francis de Sales

How can you be patient with yourself today?

"If you desire healing,
let yourself fall ill,
let yourself fall ill."

Jalaluddin Rumi

What lengths are you willing to go for healing?

"When I discover who I am, I'll be free."

Ralph Ellison

Who are you?

"The most fatal thing a man can do is try to stand alone."

Carson McCullers

Who is with you?

"Return, O my soul, to your rest; for the Lord has
dealt bountifully with you."

Psalm 116

How?

"Mental pain is less dramatic than physical pain,
but it is more common and also more hard to bear.
The frequent attempt to conceal mental pain increases
the burden: it is easier to say, "My tooth is aching"
than to say, "My heart is broken."

C.S. Lewis, The Problem of Pain

What might you be hiding?

"Someone I loved once gave me a box full of darkness. It took me years to understand that this, too, was a gift."

Mary Oliver

Open your box.

"The truth will set you free, but first it will piss you off."

Joe Kales, Twelve Steps to Happiness

Are you angry enough? At all? At who? At what?

"Expose yourself to your deepest fear; after that, fear has no power, and the fear of freedom shrinks and vanishes. You are free."

Jim Morrison

How might you do that today?

"The truth will set you free. But not until it is finished with you."

David Foster Wallace, Infinite Jest

What else is there?

"Long is the way and hard, that out of Hell leads up to light."

John Milton, Paradise Lost

Where are you at on the journey?

"We must be free not because we claim freedom,
but because we practice it."

William Faulkner

How can you practice freedom?

"Freedom is what we do with what is done to us."

Jean-Paul Sartre

Is this the same as the practice of freedom? Or is it a practice in perspective?

"Letting go gives us freedom, and freedom is the only condition for happiness. If, in our heart, we still cling to anything - anger, anxiety, or possessions - we cannot be free."

Thich Nhat Hanh

What are you clinging to?

"And after you have suffered a little while, the God of all grace, who has called you to his eternal glory in Christ, will himself restore, confirm, strengthen, and establish you."

1 Peter 5:10

Do you honestly expect full restoration in the future? Full peace?

"I wonder if that's how darkness wins, by convincing us to trap it inside ourselves, instead of emptying it out. I don't want it to win."

Jasmine Warga

Are you holding your depression captive?

"But a caged bird stands on the grave of dreams, his shadow shouts on a nightmare scream. His wings are clipped and his feet are tied so he opens his throat to sing."

Maya Angelou

Sing.

"I slept and dreamt that life was joy. I awoke and saw that life was service. I acted and behold, service was joy."

Rabindranath Tagore

Where are joy and service at in your life?

"In the heartfelt mercy of our God, the dawn from on high will visit us, to shine on those sitting in darkness, in the shadow of death, to guide our feet to the way of peace."

Anonymous

What part does spirituality play in your life?

"Any problems created by the left hand of man,
Can also be solved with the right,"

Suzy Kassem

How might you be your own solution?

"Our wounds are often the openings into the best
and most beautiful part of us."

David Richo

What beauty can you see in your depression?

"You are wrong if you think Joy emanates only or principally from human relationships. God has placed it all around us. It is in everything and anything we might experience. We just have to have the courage to turn against our habitual lifestyle and engage in unconventional living."

Jon Krakauer

Would you be courageous enough to pursue joy? If so, how?

Questions & Prompts: *Writing for Understanding*

> *"Life is filled with unanswered questions, but it is the courage to seek those answers that continues to give meaning to life. You can spend your life wallowing in despair, wondering why you were the one who was led towards the road strewn with pain, or you can be grateful that you are strong enough to survive it."*

J.D. Stroube

I have been in counseling for as long as I can remember. The long line of therapists and counselors are extensive; I have sat in on support groups, laid down on cliched couches and completed hundreds of pages of paperwork and intake forms and treatment plans. I have talked about my problems for more hours with more therapists than I can count.

All the good ones, the ones who were worth their degrees, asked questions. Tons of them. In fact, most of the sessions that stuck with me and gave me any kind of insight into my struggles were question filled. They asked, I spoke. Nothing more.

Those inquisitive helpers led our conversations with both intention and free-flowing ease. All the insights and moments of clarity that I got from talking with them came from the thoughts that their questions raised. They did not give trite or biased or even blatant advice. They gave opportunity for exploration, which was way more effective.

One of the most endearing counselors I had was when I was 7 or 8 years old. I had not spoken for close to a year because of my mother's death. I remember that as we talked and he tried to get me to open up to him, either I wouldn't or couldn't verbalize my feelings. My voice felt caged. It was when he handed me a composition notebook and a pencil and told me to do something that I have been doing ever since, that I found any kind of freedom.

He told me to "write until I felt better."

I remember going home after my sessions and finally being able to journal about everything we talked about and every question he had asked. When my voice couldn't interact with the questions, my pen could. I was able to move from silence, to written freedom to finally being able to share my journal with this man of service. Simple questions, asked in intentional and meaningful ways and through a medium that my heart could handle, brought insight into my life and gave me my voice back.

Unfortunately, I have also experienced some very straightforward, fundamental counselors. People of conservative backgrounds, they were those who wanted to fix the problem with preprogrammed solutions and cookie cutter prescriptions. They used approaches that were sometimes biased, formulaic and not client centered. These were tough experiences; I often felt disempowered and at the mercy of someone else providing the solution for the darkness I was carrying.

I believe in allowing my personal writing practice to function the same way as the question asking counselors. The same way my favorite counselor did. Through inquiry. Through innovation in approach. I think that while straightforward, linear advice can sometimes have its place, as well as seem more natural to the human experience (fulfilling our desire to save and be saved), it is the art, practice and cultivation of query and exploration that really brings us into lasting change and hope. In my darkest of days, it is the will to explore what it is that I feel, understand, see and don't see that gives continued hope.

These questions and prompts will ask something of you. Dive deep.

An Open Letter

What do you have to say to your depression and grief? Consider it a person or a being and let it know exactly how you feel, both about it and about yourself because of it.

A Goodbye Letter
In tandem with your open letter, what release/goodbye do you need to give? Speak candidly and let it know what your separation from it will look like.

What do you need to forgive your loved one for?

What is?

What can be?

If you could talk to your loved one today, what
would you say to them?

What is the kindest thing you can do for yourself
today? Tomorrow? The next?

What does the expression "never turn away" mean to you, and how will you do that no matter what?

Thinking about your life right now, what is true?
What is a lie?

What is the hardest part of living with loss?

How are you different from others who are mourning? How might you be the same?

What do you need to hear?

Set a timer for 5 min and close your eyes. When time is up, answer this question:

What did you see?

What are some of the most profound lessons your
loved one taught you?

What is the sweetest thing you have ever known?

What do you wish for your loved one?

What do you hope for yourself?

What is something helpful someone once said to you that you have remembered ever since? Write about that and why it stuck with you.

What might you need to embrace right now?

Who do you care about? Write about them.

What are you passionate about? What gets you fired up?

Why did you pick up this book?

If you had no limitations, no restrictions and a solid guarantee of success, what would you be doing today?

Can you describe a time in your life when you were
most happiest?

What does your voice sound like?

What are your morning and evening routines?
What can you change about them to feel happier?

What would be different about the world if you had
never been born?

How would you like to be remembered?

What keeps you moving when you really don't want to?

What have you done right?

What would you like your children/those coming
after you to know about you? About life?

What did you learn from your loved on that leads to living well, being happy or honoring values you hold?

Imagine a life without grief or depression. How would you feel? What would you be able to accomplish?

Do you agree with this statement? "Pain can be prideful."
Why or why not?

What gave your loved one strength or resilience to
stand firm through the trials of life?

Think about someone you know who has also dealt with grief and/or depression. What can you learn from them about living with loss?

What would it mean for you to suffer well?

How do you remember your loved one?

Are you afraid of what love demands?

What is the thing that makes you want to put your
pen down right now?

How have you changed over the past year? The Past
5 years? Since yesterday?

Place a picture of your loved one in your mind.
What do you believe about them?

In what way have you given up fighting?

What is your ideal world?

What can you do to help make that world a reality?

If that ideal world is an impossibility, how do you think you might thrive and live despite that fact?

Rock Bottom: Where is it?

What do you believe about loss?

What is the opposite of lonely?

Are you selfish? Self-indulgent?
How?

What is forgiveness?

What might your loved one have wanted for you right now? Tomorrow? Ten years from now?

What is your heart saying right now?

Are you a victim?

Or are you a survivor?

What are you willing to do for love?

What are you not willing to do for love?

What was the happiest moment of your life?

What memories of your loved one makes you smile?
Write about them all.

Who are the influential people in your life, dead or alive? What did they teach you?

What is your next step?

What are your priorities for life?

For This Year?

For This Month?

For Today?

For this moment?

What drains you?

What gives you life?

What in this life is calling you? Elaborate.

Lists: *Writing for Fact*

> *A well-ordered life is like climbing a tower; the view halfway up is better than the view from the base, and it steadily becomes finer as the horizon expands.*

William Lyons Phelps

I spent nine months of my life as a resident of a ministry with a therapeutic, addiction, mental health focus. I enrolled there with the purpose of finding stability in my life, behavior and spirit.

While I was there, I will never forget meeting a tall, skinny man from Michigan who started off as a resident of the facility and later, became a counselor. His name was Nathan. In many ways, I saw myself in much of his struggles and personality. Introspective and introverted, I think that we were both very internal people. While I didn't have the privilege of continuing my relationship with this man beyond my time there, he taught me a very valuable skill that I have carried with me: to be thankful in all things. To be grateful for all that I had, had experienced and had been given. And he did this in a very unique, systematic way. (I think systemic approaches sometimes benefit introverts because it is the opposite of how we approach life. Systems versus emotion.)

Nathan taught me to count my blessings. Literally. He taught me to take pen and paper and to every day, make an intentionally long list of all that I was grateful for. And not only was this list to be long, it was to be unique each and every day.

Now, it must be said that I am not a methodical person. AT ALL. My home is not extremely organized, and I don't lean towards a life of symmetry. At home, I know where everything is and how to access things when I need them but if someone were to ask me about my system, I would not know how to respond. The one I have is deeply personal. It only makes sense to me.

If I am honest however, sometimes my disorganization feeds my depression. My grief finds solace in it too. When I am really lost, it is hard to think, let alone to think logically. I need something to anchor my thoughts and my heart because left to their own devices, they flounder. The messier my heart and mind get, the messier my home. The messier my home, the messier my heart and mind. Every day, I must make a consistent, conscious effort to reign in my thoughts, to believe what is true and to see exactly what is in front of me. I must consciously decide to clean myself up. For those who suffer from depression, thinking and believing (and living) in concrete ways like this can have positive effects on long term wellness. For all of us who grieve, dominion over the things we can touch can give a sense of control.

This way of being is the opposite of the question-centric counselors and the open-ended writing prompts I have come to love. Over the years, I was introduced to a different form of writing that has been just as immensely helpful, if not more. Nathan introduced to the art of the list.

When you make a list with a therapeutic focus, whether it be a gratitude list or something else, you are consciously asking yourself to recognize those things that are factual, measurable and therapeutic for your soul. The things they produce may either be negative or positive. However, when you take the time to engage them for whatever they may be, you might begin to perceive that which is true and noble and secure. The tangible things that can be counted on and believed.

50 different names for the word "love".

50 things you believe.

40 things you never want to forget.

20 Things you want to stop doing.

21 ways your loved one made you smile.

45 reasons to live.

20 more.

25 positive sentences that start with "I am..."

5 things you remember about the one you lost.

10 more.

15 more.

20.

List all the turning points in your life.

5 lies you currently believe.

5 absolute truths.

List your achievements.

List your failures.

Name 10 things that make you happy.

12 resolutions for the next 12 months.

100 words that describe your loved one.

List all your disappointments.

All your regrets.

40 ways you can live despite your failures and regrets.

5 risks you are determined to take in the future.

365 things you are grateful for.

Every person you love.

The Never List
Write 100 sentences that begin with the words
"_____ never." (Fill in the _____ with your loved
one's name.)

The Always List
Write 100 sentences that begin with the words
"_____ always". (Fill in the _____ with your loved
one's name.)

The Hope List
Write 101 sentences that begin with the words "I hope".

Write a list explaining all the ways to be happy.

1000 things You Love about Yourself. or Someone
You Love
(If you can't name 1000, stop. Go live out some new reasons.
Then come back and work on your list.)

Words: *Writing for Definition*

"As you simplify your life, the laws of the universe will be simpler; solitude will not be solitude, poverty will not be poverty, nor weakness weakness."

Henry David Thoreau

I have always thought that depression is anything but simple. In my experience, and to the contrary, the confusing chaos and lethargy depression creates is anything but simple or trite.

I received a formal mental health diagnosis in my late 20's. For some reason, none of the counselors that had come before had put the words "Major Depressive Disorder, Recurring" on a piece of paper with my name at the top. Now, my fate was sealed with a label. It was also the first time I was offered medication. By that time, my head was so messed up that I was willing to do any and everything for just a little bit of relief (the meds helped).

So, there I was. A sad, 29-year-old black man sitting in the office of a psychiatrist with a thick Indian accent, being offered pills for the first time. In a room full of framed degrees, well-worn books and the smell of patchouli in the air, the doctor went on and on explaining side effects and dosages and the importance of weekly talk therapy to compliment the medication.

As I sat there, all I could think of was how confused I was. How I was utterly lost in the conversation. I had no clue what I was doing there, what he was talking about and what was going on. There were too many clinical words and long explanations and multisyllabic vocabulary hanging in the air. I was willing to take the medication but didn't know what I felt about it. I was glad to finally have a label and name, but I also hated it. I was tired and confused. And for some reason, hungry.

I went home that afternoon wildly unhinged. Having no idea at all about what the hell was going on. I was appreciative of finding help but out of everything that was said, the only solace I found was in the label. "Major Depressive". It was not as if the label changed my chemistry but it felt important because I needed definition. Those two small, seemingly insignificant words were easy to understand. They were a starting point for jumping into understanding more about myself, slowly. They were not attached to a long series of sentences that were hard to interpret and they were utterly and completely bite sized. I could chew on them and unpack them as and when I needed.

I took the medication. I participated in the talk therapy. Additionally, I began to journal around basic words. I learned that I could take very small points of understanding and expand upon them as I needed and wanted. I learned that I did not have to embrace all of the confusion that comes with being depressed or filled with loss. I could focus on that which is most easily understood and begin climbing out of the deep end of the pool from there. My relationship with counselors changed from that point on, as did the relationship with how I wrote and processed.

My relationship with grief changed as well. When I began to simplify, I began to understand that my feelings could be better engaged when I knew what was in front of me. When I could clearly define my sadness. Even when I was planning my father's funeral, it was simplicity that kept me going, not confusion or uncertainty.

These words are for you. Chew on them slowly. Use them to write from whatever place is most easily understood. With ease, write as you will.

Abandoned

Resolve

Hide

Ceremony

Trauma

Survive

Grief

Cold

Ghostly

Invisible

Limp

Down

Hatred

Fragile

Blame

Dull-edged

Memory

Encaged

Fly

Light

Strong

You

We

Me

Early

Always.

Forever.

Faith

Fear.

Ease.

Satisfaction.

Sweat.

Joy

Cure

Heart

Flesh

Water

Blood.

Soul

High

Higher

Brittle

Defeated

Empty

Order

Irrational

Lonely

Shame

Wounded

Wronged

Rejected

Dead

Bone

Paradise

Misery

Hell

Heaven

For More Information

Therapeutic writing. Memoir. End of Life Discussions. Mental Health.

If you are interested in these topics and are looking for content, resources, encouragement and the like, sign up for Garrett's newsletter. You will receive it by email twice monthly, plus some information on my other books and resources available. You can check at Garrett's main website as well as Beyond Morning for additional content.

For Garrett's Newsletter
Sign Up Here
For Garrett's Personal Site go to
www.garrettdrewellis.com
For end of life and memoir services go to
www.beyondmorning.org

Acknowledgements

<u>I owe the following people a debt of gratitude in the writing and shaping of this book. Your kindness and friendship have been immeasurable.</u>

Andi Cumbo-Floyd: Some people exist in this world as those called to encourage. To spur those around them on toward the fulfillment of inherent capability. You my friend, have been that for me. Without you, andilit and the community you have created, I don't know if I would be the writer I am today. Thank you.

To the man I call *"The Unnamed Counselor"*: You changed my life at a time when I thought all was lost. The mantra you instilled in me is the namesake of this book. I do not remember your name but you will forever be etched on the surface of my heart. Thank you.

Dayona, Jair, Jireh, Joy and Jaxon: No one knows what it is like to support a person struggling with grief and depression like you do. Thank you for being present as I navigate my process. You were there when I was writing myself through many of these prompts. Love you always.

About The Author

Garrett Drew Ellis began writing therapeutically at the age of 7 years old and professionally at 21. A ghostwriter, author and mentor, Garrett believes that writing is first and foremost a healing modality. "Publishing and being in print is great" Garrett says, "But feeling and hearing one's voice through the written word is a much more valuable experience."

Owner of Beyond Morning LLC, Garrett is a writer and end of Life Doula who helps individuals tell their life's story and navigate the end of their days. Garrett has written over 30 books and memoirs on behalf of others and lives with his wife and children in Central Pennsylvania. You can find out more about his work and writing at beyondmorning.org and garrettdrewellis.com

Made in the
USA
Middletown, DE